The Uncanny Valley

Poems by Jennifer Martelli

ISBN: 978-0-9969887-5-9

Printed in the United States of America

Cover Design: Tracey Ranauro
Front and Back Cover Photos: Tracey Ranauro

Also by Jennifer Martelli:

Apostrophe

Big Table Publishing Company
Boston, MA
www.bigtablepublishing.com

For
Vin, Mia, and Michael
And for my parents

Table of Contents

HE

Elysian   13
Peasant's Pie, Devil's Tooth   14
On Sex Chromosomes and Co-Dependency   15
Fear of Going Blind is the Fear of Castration   16
Supper During Watergate   17
The Veiled Women   18
Bomb   19
Kind Hearted Woman   20
"Peace and Trust Can Win the Day Despite
    of All Your Losing"   21

HE and I

At a Crowded Party, I Am Not Envious   25
Heaviness   26
Wrists   27
Honeymoon at the End of the Eighties   28
Pumpjacks in Iran   29
Colostrum   30
Incus. Maleus. Stapes. (Hammer. Anvil. Stirrup.)   31
Paean   32
Coleus   33
Ananke   34
Strep   35
Zeus Re-Creating the World   36
Similes After a Quick Thaw and a Cold Snap   37
"The heart dies without a space for love, without
    a moral horizon"   38
Over a Pu Pu Platter   39

THEY

    Tree   43

    The Mountain, 1971   44

    Tit   45

    Evil Fields   46

    Thistle, Blue   47

    Wreaths the Elected Wear   48

    Day of Atonement   50

    Mr. Golub's Death   51

    Bleshazzar's Feast   52

    Gephyrophobia (Fear of Crossing Bridges)   53

    State of Deseret   54

    Prayer of the Last Baby Boomer to the Madonna
        de la Soccorso   55

SHE

    At the End of the Visible Spectrum   59

    Austerlitz   60

    Seated Figure with Hat   61

    Woman Making Omens on the Second Floor   62

    Psychopomps   63

    The Girl with Black, Black Hair and
        the Golden Snake   64

    Silhouette   66

    Sisters, Braiding   67

    Dog Days   68

    Festival of the Eclipse   69

    Stone Formations Along the Marginal Way   70

    Fox Sisters   71

SHE and I

    The Ruins of Rievaulx Abbey   75

    No Face   76

    Singer   77

    A Mother of Dolls   78

    Wives   80

    Picture of a Botched Abortion   82

    Avocado   83

    Orlando Poem   84

    Feeding the Carnivorous Plant   85

    Miacento   86

    But the Buddha is Kind; Life is Always a Balancing
        Out   87

    Hump, or "The Weight of Life is Heavier
        Than Even the Weight of Things"   88

    Phantom   89

    Joan Mitchell Mulls a Possible Mandibulectomy   90

    Dissolution of the Soviet Union   91

    Aphrodisiums   92

I

    Apostrophe   95

    The Range   96

    As a Crow Flies   97

    They Fall, Each Day, Think of It   98

    Cocaine, the Last Night   99

    A Fall   100

    God as a Tiger in a Cage   101

    Siren   102

    Unfounded, Ungrounded   103

    Smoking Outside in Front of a Motion Sensor Light
        Because I Love My Children   104

    The Tao of Virgil Sollozzo   105

    The Devil Tides   106

    Ultrasound of a Ghost   107

    After God   108

    Mal'Occhio   109

    White Birches   110

"Oh mother-eye, oh mother-eye, crush me in."
~ Anne Sexton

HE

Elysian

In the movie, the men of the town
sit dumb as oxen in a New England backwater, drunk,

while their women-folk meet in a secret glen
with a city-boy they lured there.

They drug him and fuck him and then they slit his throat
for good crops. Somehow, at sometime, God

grew a penis and a beard. The men
in the movie can never tell of this rite, or their eyes

and tongues will be ripped out with shears and sewn shut
with neat stitches. After, the women quilt and the men plow

or build barns. A psychic once told me
I have no male energy, and I have friends who boast

that they think like a man, which is confusing to me
what with their broken hearts. In the movie

the men are complicit in their women's
Neolithic pagan Mafia. The crops bear no blight.

My father had no sons. Somehow and at sometime
God grew a penis. Men seem to me

long-suffering, carrying their crosses
trying to rid themselves of the women they conceive.

Peasant's Pie, Devil's Tooth

He wasn't the body yet.
Joanie and I spoke over him, from each side
of the bed in ICU and Uncle Billy was at the foot.
We spoke of food, of the seven fishes
on Christmas Eve, all the shrimps and lobster and smelts,
of zepoli and how the uncles cooked.
They're long gone, as well as their accents.

We're good Americans and eternal
Catholics. You'd have to unravel both strands
from our DNA. We had laid out my father's blue blazer and
flag lapel pin, his red and blue striped tie.
But there was still time :
the heart monitor metronomed and
the oxygen sighed and sighed and we talked

over him of food until that silence
that falls every twenty minutes or so
when one of two things happens: an angel
walks through the room, or the whole world stops
silent to remember when President Lincoln
was shot. It's in our DNA,

see? American and Catholic,
we'd pause, honoring and awed:
fra diavlo, pizza ghiena, pupa con luova.
They'd drawn the drapes on the glass walls.
There were no more emergencies for him.
We talked like sin eaters over my father's body:
egg bread, we mean, *peasant's pie, devil's tooth.*

On Sex Chromosomes and Co-dependency

But what is this Y
but a tiny broken X!

He is hobbled, one leg broke
off, (not even a peg) poor limping soldier,

and oh needing the crutch
that is the X, and X

shoulders him and weeps and needs
his need or she will die:

unduplicated, an untied knot
opened, and the helix unraveled.

No kisses, not a single kiss.
That is the crux.

Fear of Going Blind is the Fear of Castration

In the uncanny
valley men wear goats'
horns painted black, gold and red
around their thick necks
so the witches who
try to curse them are tricked by
what they see as so
many phalluses
and, distracted, fly right
into each other.

Supper During Watergate

My father sat at the head of the table, dusky
      as Nixon's five o'clock shadow–he glared
at my older sister who would not look at him,
      would not look up or pull
her straight black hair away from her face (I had yet to give up my
stretchy headbands, and the baby was still in pig tails then).
      Supper during Watergate
was not much different than any other supper, except that
      one night I hid
the microphone of a cassette tape player between the copper mugs
my mother lined on the shelf,
                    cups so unsafe to use, the oxide
leached into the fronds of the spider ferns she planted. She hung
the copper tray above the dinner table and it glowed
like a penny tossed down a well.
          In Korea, it is believed that ghosts
will come to the sound of chopsticks clicking porcelain bowls,
they are so hungry, they will just mill around, waiting. They will come
even if they hear your teeth click.
             That was the sound we heard
when I played the tape back before dessert: and the hum of the tape
circling and the sound of the hearings from the television.
My father loved the President then as I love the President now.
He felt victimized as Nixon and when he got up without
asking to be excused he spilt his water all over the table: the knots
in the wood grew long under the drops and they looked to me like
sad faces. My mother, sweet and reaching
      as Rose Mary Wood, stretched
across to wipe up the mess. *It's Watergate*, she said. She said
I shouldn't upset him even more.

The Veiled Women

walking along Broadway from the bakery and
sometimes, the new burka store, got my father nervous.

I'd drive him by the Beach, by
St. Theresa's: *well, I won't be going there anymore*, he'd point,

screwed by God, by my mother's Alzheimer's, his cancer:
      he was going to die and
my mother wouldn't know. The Church sold off St. Theresa's

to pay for legal fees and the stone cross was pulled down like the statue
of Saddam Hussein–roped and toppled. They glued
      a crescent moon

to the terra cotta brick and now it's something else.
A woman waits out front, so veiled all I see are her eyes,
      like my own black coon cat.

Her eyes don't scare me, though: if you live here long enough,
no one will meet your gaze. My father hated cats, too.
      A man may die

once he has married three daughters off, Rumi said.
      My two sisters and I
feed our cats til they're fat. My own cat's fur grows long

and she sits waiting, covered and purring, her eyes
green or golden, kissing me with her eyes, warm and plump under
      fur that covers her
            like a black niqab.

Bomb

After they started the morphine drip after they took out
       the breathing tubes
and the nurses left us

I lay my head net to his on his pillow
for I'd heard that I'd never be so near to God
       as when He came for the dying.

One of us had to be high to be this close to each other--
when we danced at my wedding, there I was,

so drunk! And here my father lay,
an old undetonated bomb, and I, waiting crouching and cautious:

because this was God's last shot with me.
What time he passed, I can't say because the clocks
       moved back an hour.

Kind-Hearted Woman

The dead make do, like hobos. He used his eyes for coin,
    the silver toll
to cross that trestle in the old freight that chugged
through my dark tunnel just after midnight. He came back
    older, viral

and ashamed. Even in death, ashamed, and still mean.
I had hoped to make cave paintings in my belly,
a warm Lascaux: a man traced on a wall, wounded, gored.

You were the one who liked to cook, he said. *So cook.*
But I sketched an ancient Madonna, smudged her privates
    with my thumb.

In the morning, I found the ghost had drawn,
    with his gray bones, a cat
on the stone foundation of my house
by the driveway, by the tomato pots left out too long into the fall.

"Peace and Trust Can Win the Day Despite of All Your Losing"
~ Robert Plant, "Immigrant Song"

This time, when he came back, he rose out of a puddle of meat
        drippings by the grill.
Engulfed in smoke from the white coals, I almost missed him,
        being dead and all,

he was tired and his hands had fallen asleep so he had to fling them
to get my attention, using his old deltoids, clumsy. *You're fading* he said

ashamed for me. I was hot as a Pict woman, all blue tattooed in sweat
waving my spatula: *I'm sorry,*

I didn't mean for that to happen! But he was already sinking back down
like a birth reversed, uninterested in this world, my world.
        If I've learned

nothing, hard as it seems to be dead, the dead don't care,
don't miss us for long.

HE and I

At a Crowded Party, I am not Envious

of the beautiful woman who walks behind me—
her thick auburn hair, almost round eyes,
and breasts I couldn't buy. There's a man
coming toward me, yes, but his eyes
are fixed on her promised land.
I am as meaningless
as a sea to this Moses—

he parts me and the crowd with a brush
of his hand, the back of his hand pressed
against my arm which has thus been touched

by complete want and adoration much
in the same way I've hoped God looks at me:

I would walk in front of a beautiful woman
one hundred thousand times to be moved like that.

Heaviness

The wet snow split the Japanese cherry tree in half
and that broken half landed on my car in the driveway.

Later, the town's tree guy came with a chainsaw
and sawed that poor half tree into bits, with its innards all
        splayed and white.

We both smoked a cigarette from my pack.
Then he hoisted his chain and chainsaw and told me not to hope
        for blooms in spring.

He didn't have to tell me that he'd fathered only girls, though he did.
I knew before he spoke of his plight.

You know how? I wanted him so bad,
I wanted him so bad to like me.

Wrists

I married that man because of his wrists.
They were thick—one width from crook to hand—
and that had meaning to me. Archaic wedding bands
were metal cuffs wound around a bride's wrist.
Wrist, like wrest, can be sexual or violent;
like writ, a law, a forcing, constraint,
thus handcuffs around the wrists, and well,
violence and sex,
if that's the way it is, and that's always
the way it is. I've read many books regarding the crucifixion.
Christ was nailed through his wrists,
just above, through the tough
sinews, the stringy part that would keep him
up long enough to suffocate. Again, laws,
constraint. And the women! Weeping at his feet!
Stigmatics have been getting it wrong, and so hysteria
can be forced by an image seen over and over enough times,
and hysteria, with its Greek root, roaming womb, and womb
like wound, like woo, like woe seems a circular thing.
The pulse in the wrist
is much like the heartbeat of a stray cat, the one
you lure with milk in a tuna can, lift, toss
out of your back yard. But it's a boney wrist
at that, and fitting only for a woman.

Honeymoon at the End of the Eighties

Three martello towers stood round and abandoned on a dried field within the walls of Old Quebec City. There were no wars anymore, no need for garrisons, no need to hide men. (My new name meant hammer, too, or little hammer: his sister wanted me to share a surname with her, or she felt this was important, after a night of cocaine, when everything was manic and important.) Later, at the Argentinian steakhouse, below the sidewalk, where the walls were brick and cool, he and I ate raw meat and potato shoestrings. I wore chunky necklaces: fat, fake rubies, glass emeralds and topaz. My poor body was sore. The clitoris, aroused and exposed, was described once as a tower or hill housing termites, made of red mud and spit. The cold ground seeped through my cracked Doc Marten's, made my legs ache in tight jeans—you'd think we did it right there, on the field, on my military coat (the one with shoulder pads like a tin soldier.)

Pumpjacks in Iran

And worse, this drinking bird cannot get its fill: it tips
up and down, sipping the dry Texas earth. Or maybe the dry

plains outside of Tehran. Think of all the dinosaurs down there,
liquid. Think of a fly dead in amber. Or in a jar

of honey on a kitchen table, made mellow yet bright by the sun.
The long-haired black cat watches through her fur the fly sink deep

down into the golden sweetness. In a million years,
a man will give his love a ring of amber with the fossil

of a fly in the middle. He will have the stone set in white
gold, or rose yellow. The young girl will look up shy,

modest. The man has a heart broken in two tattooed
on the nape of his neck even his mother hasn't seen.

The ring will never taste of honey, but the gesture is
lovely. The couple lives in a ghost town, the life blood

long dried, the people moved away, the churches and the bars,
the minarets, warehouses where they square-danced
        are mostly abandoned.

Colostrum

The dinosaurs in the movie are cloned female,
certain hormones suppressed, and yet

some mutate into males,
and they breed. They are hungry

all the time. I've never been
so large as now. I make cleavage

watching TV next to my husband,
mindlessly touch and press

my own breasts beneath his faded
red chamois shirt.

The drop of clear pre-milk
satisfies no one's ache. It is

tasteless. He licks the tip of my finger,
You're a mammal, he says,

and almost looks relieved.

Incus. Malleus. Stapes. (Anvil. Hammer. Stirrup.)

What makes you a mammal is your ear: the three bones deep
down the canal that you and I and the sea cow and the vole and rapist
have and one bone looks like an anvil in a blacksmith's shop.

The Greeks and Romans worshipped a blacksmith as a god. But
a lame god, marred and ugly, thrown down to earth by his parents.
If he couldn't hold his mother, he'd hold a hammer, our other bone,

and you can hear him pound like a molten river, over and over against
        the anvil: he makes the metal
malleable, hot and soft and hot and soft and blue and finally useful:
stirrups to mount the animal you'll escape on.

More than the warm milk from your mother's nipple, the wet birth,
the fur, it's the rejected god,
all sullen as a volcano, all atoil that I hear.

Paean

You came canted like a drunk uncle
looming big as a mountain. If the mountain
did come, did it come
as you did: slowly, like play,
tossing handfuls of small stones
at my feet so that, yes, I did
dance and dance and dance
over and over calling your name?

Coleus

I felt the rain before it fell, like menses,
salty-aired and swollen as my upper lip, like the sweat
on your upper lip.

The coleus on the table between us turned deep pink
in the last rays of sunlight, its leaves all pink tongues—they
trembled when I leaned in to get close to you.

I wanted you to see how my heartbeat traveled through
        the tabletop to the plant,
but your eyes dilated too wide
and you circled my wrist

with both hands to get me to see you. You didn't see
the coleus. You never saw what happened. You told me I'd get wet,
soaked and I do, I know. I did.

Ananke, Greek Goddess of Necessity

Necessity itself a loose
word, an ancient loopy god, it means

constriction, the way an indifferent green
anaconda takes you in its coils.

Necessity, a noose
shaped like a sacrificial wreath,

and the shape of our lips when we breath
just before we are about to kiss.

I prefer the linear and like things to unwind.

When I've waited too long, I begin to unravel
the strands, unbraid the rope, untie the knot.

There is nothing kind
about an inevitable and personal

god.

Strep

I've sent my husband down the cellar to play The Who
then Elvis Costello then Velvet Underground. Sent him

down with the cat. We'll never leave that rotten decade,
I say. I've cooked all day, heavy fatty foods. Bought rock

salt, bags of it, poured it over my front steps as the plow
scrapes the dry street. My heart is drawn to what's left on the pitch.

There's barely enough snow to call it tv static. The street lamps'
strange ovals I confused with the moon, that little camel's hump.

Don't trust me. I am not trustworthy: not because I'm from this
angry state but because I like the closing in. The clouds

sag with the weight of snow. Like a uterine wall, they need to let go,
bleed out something cold, then we'll see what's left. If the sky

reflects an interior life, this is a dull one. Nothing toxic, nothing, not
even yoga or crystal has ever relieved me for long. An eye

is supposed to open in the middle of my brow. The snowy weight
hurts, gives me an ice spike, and I taste cold knives when I swallow.

Zeus Re-Creating the World

He got scared and swallowed everything in the world: the lakes and
    trees, mountains, homes.
He swallowed the universe, too, fearing usurption (just like his father,
    who ate all his kids.)
He choked (like his father did), spit out
everything in the world: the lakes and trees, mountains, homes,
children, other gods but this time everything was coated and wet.
What I mean is that there was order in the world, even the fear
    seemed manageable.

That is how I came to love you, after you swallowed me
    and I flowed in you
like molten copper in the cast of your perfect form, like a cold hand
inched by the teeth into a leather glove.

I have your taste on me now all the time.

Similes After a Quick Thaw and a Cold Snap

I heard thunder last night
when the cold lay over the warmth–
thunder like a visitor stamping his feet on my porch.

I saw lightning through my window
like a police car flashing out front.

In the morning, the snow had fallen once again,
covering the cars and bushes and
old Christmas trees on the sidewalk.

I think of you all the time,
which is to say, I think of myself.

I saw tinsel woven and poking through a pile of snow
and I made a wish because it shone all silver
like a star.

I heard an icicle crack like a Pyrex dish
above me on the eave of my home.

When I looked where the icicle had fallen, it lay in the sun
broken off, blue and whole.
Like a will, like a heart.

Oh, Lord, I am the great diminisher.
So often, I just miss you.

"The heart dies without space for love, without a moral horizon"

~ after Yehuda Amachai

I came upon a heart, lying on octagon tiles
in the foyer of an apartment, beneath the mailboxes.
I came upon a dark-haired girl's lung punctured. I heard a cat
in heat or fighting: one thing could be another.
I came upon my heart bouncing on taut sheets back into my fist.
I came upon my heart punching through a twig cage.

The moon rises later each day, but gets caught
in the shaking maple's branches.

I turned and came upon my husband lying next to me in bed.
I was one parentheses and he was the other
      in the middle of a white sentence.
So I say, *it's like the whole sky has turned its big old back on me*
(he asks if I have anyone to talk to). I say, *I came upon the moon*
trying to catch my eye, doing things so I'd look up, and you
I'm talking to you.

Over a Pu Pu Platter

I assure you
that nothing I did was done from spite
or meanspiritedness.

I want to remind you now

of circling the stones
at Stonehenge
that time when we could cross
a country in just days.

You've known all along
what I'm made up of.
We're too old
for forgiveness.

THEY

Tree

The hand says: I did not plant that tree.

I did not heft the noose over its branch, test its weight.

My brown eyes say: I did not see because it was so dark.

I did not see that man lying on the sidewalk.

My mouth forms the words: I am not racist or it is wrong.

Something in me is old. It is not from this country.

Something in me is new. It is American. It is my heart.

My tongue says: This is the only language I know.

My tongue says: This is the only language I know.

My feet wonder: Are we from the low country of America?

I can smell the ocean from my back yard.

My hair says: I look like everybody I ever grew up with.

I look like everybody off the boat. From the old country.

I could smell the ocean from over there too. Many people

mostly men are angry at me, they say my new heart bleeds.

The fist says: I am not burying anything with this shovel.

I am planting a tree.

The Mountain, 1971

The boys threw rocks to keep us away from them
because their hair felt too good in our fists and we liked
to run at them and pin them down, we liked

how they cried when we punched too hard. Once,
Johnny (or maybe Tony, he was a nice boy),
pulled a handkerchief to surrender.

He ran off crying, too.
Once, Diane got hit in the neck with a broken bottle.
That got us mad. And the boys looked scared.

Our new ranch-style homes were close enough for us to hear
the daily body count on TV
through the back screen doors.

The whole neighborhood was built on an old pig farm.
The dirt from all those foundations they piled higher and higher,
home after home, until we called it The Mountain.

We would find broken things there–tea saucers, cups–once,
a bone we hoped was human, but was from a pig.
My mother wouldn't let me bring it inside to boil off clean and white.

Sometimes, at recess we planned A War there and this is how it went:
say, five boys against five girls, no kung fu. We'd fight in the skirts
we'd worn that day. The boys wanted it as much as we did.
For the year The Mountain stood, we outweighed them all.

Tit

In the strip of cream skin between her bra and silky slip, the mole
beneath my mother's right breast scared me: I sat on her bed
      with my dolls and peeked.
Hanging from the corner of her bureau mirror were rosary beads,
black peas you could finger as you prayed.
I drew Miss America sashes on my dolls, Barbie,
      and Francie, and Midge,
with thick magic marker–a slash over their breasts,
across the stomachs
      to their snap-on hips.

The stain wouldn't come off, even when they floated in the pink tub
and I rubbed and rubbed the hard nubby plastic with my thumb.
Their feet, up on tip-toes en pointe, had my teeth marks clean through
      to the wire that allowed my dolls to kneel.

My father sat in the den across the hall, manipulating the rabbit ears
      on the tv
to catch the signal from the aerial on the chimney where crows
perched cawing: *I saw! I saw! I saw!*

Evil Fields

Living and building on a veneer of sugar and strawberries
         over oatmeal.
Walking on bowls of oatmeal.

All of Florida hollowed out by sinkholes.
Whole homes swallowed, or just one room.

A man was swallowed so fast, his brother
heard him screaming from below, heard

the television still on down there, the cord plugged into the wall.
He heard him howl. And then not killed–gone. A whole

field in Rome, too, honeycombed
by hundreds of tombs and every woman

put in alive.
Every woman given one lamp, one bowl of milk.

A whole field compromised. An empire. A whole
state, a panhandle, a peninsula.

Weakened. Folks
put in the ground alive and willed dead.

Thistle, Blue

Someone pulled up a bamboo grove in China and planted it here,
in the pith of Marblehead, on the foot path. Someone

found an acorn and buried it and now there's an old fat oak
whose branches cross overhead. Someone built a house

by the oak's roots and put up a fence choked
with red creeper and crow feathers and mossy hair

and there is clover and there is thistle, blue.
They hung wood chimes on their back porch and I

can hear them on warmer days though it might be
the bamboo clinking while a rabbit or a snake or

something moves through the hollow stalks. Someone hung
a paper heart in a plastic pouch, and a sheer scarf and beads strung

on a hank of yarn from the branch I pass under that fat oak:
The Blessing Tree. For the year I've vowed to walk every day

they've dangled: mold grows on the heart and it is mottled black,
the scarf torn, the beads dull. They all hang

even at night, when the owls and the bats
hunt. If I stopped, the heart and scarf and beads would hover
        just above my black hair.

Wreaths the Elected Wear

I have a wreath with six gray beach rocks glued
       on the braided willow,
rocks the size of eggs. The glue grew gummy and one
by one the rocks dropped off. I replaced that wreath

with a wreath of small speckled eggs made of hollow wood
in a tight circle. This goes up on Ash Wednesday.
Wreaths are sacred circles: inside

the circle is the sacrifice. All people can do is stand
outside of it and watch a man have a cage of bees
put on his head. Or, the wreath is a crown on the fontanel

of a virgin. No one of this earth can touch the girl.
Her hair is so black and soft, maybe it's blonde, maybe
curly and coarse as the weeping willow branches

braided to make the wreath. I have a wreath of black
crow feathers made of silken threads. I have a wreath
of tiny pine cones on shimmery white birch twigs.

I have a wreath of stars made out of tin. I have a wreath
of chili peppers, one of wild flowers picked from the garden
of a woman hanged as a witch: her garden of blue phlox and rue.

Some hang on my front door, some in my kitchen, some in the bath.
Whoever is in the sacred circle is saved for the gods,
but I think there's nothing better than seeing a good kill.

The roses' attar rose when they bent the stems to weave the crown.
I have a wreath of iron roses painted white. I hung it on a white wall
so all you see is the idea of the circle and the idea of the roses.

In a movie, a woman is in a circle of townsfolk
    who throw rocks at her
until she is dead. She holds her arms out like the hands of a clock
and then she kneels and covers her head. The woman is in the circle

her own hands make, that's how close the people are. Halos
are wreaths of light, even the martyrs tied to trees
    and shot with arrows wear them.
All we can do is stand outside the circle and watch.

Day of Atonement

Dangling from a rope on the side of my house, the man
pulls nails from his mouth and pounds.

The brown sparrow hovers to a blur all day
just beyond the chain's length holding the neighbor's dog

that idiot barks in perfect time to the hammer
until it's all one metallic bang, and

I pray that dog dead. A nail
falls from the man's mouth when he calls his hammer cunt

and lands on my porch like an awful thunderbolt
I'll kick off with my foot—tit for tat,

the nail should land perfect in the eye of a romantic
looking up to September's afternoon moon.

This year's fall much like last year's fall.

Mr. Golub's Death

Four baby ducks following their mother to Oliver Pond fell through
the sewer grates on Ruby Ave. where the old trees
        are hollow, limb by limb they molt

even without a storm: muscular arms strewn all over. We scooped
the baby ducks out with a ladle tied to a broom. The cold

air though the veins of the lone Seminole turned its leaves maroon
and orange. Mr. Golub died bleeding into his belly (I was told

he was aware and afraid.) The sparrows flew from his roof
to the hospice guy's car and back to his roof for the whole

day he died. They flew in one fractured thought, a point of view
from bad loci. My neighbors and I whispered
        from a crumbling stoop–I brewed

coffee to keep us warm while we waited through the day til
        moonrise. Good
coffee makes good neighbors: all of this in a day here is true.

Belshazzar's Feast

An old woman says her rosary while she watches Lawrence Welk,
her feet raised on the naugahyde ottoman. Black onyx beads,
moon glow plastic ones, silver plate and garnet beads, one set carved
from a tree in a grove in Israel: some dangle, some are coiled
into a red pleather snap envelope. Xanax the size of one bead
tucked under her tongue to keep her calm
while she dies. Her eyes move back and forth:
the writing is on the wall.
I take the rosaries in my fist so I don't get bit.

Now they hang still on my own bedpost. A Persian cat
howls from the porch below my window. She leaps for the moths and
the glow worms that dangle then morph into more moths.
The Persian crosses the street, cuts
her territory in half. A storm took down a giant tree
and all the wires running through it. The tree stands black,
        branchless, split
almost through to the sidewalk. The girls outside are lithe and do
handstands, scissors. The whole neighborhood stinks of burning
plastic funk and it stings our eyes: we all look
like we're crying or high.

Gephyrophobia

I call my friend Alan to talk while I drive up the coast, past
      a friend's house in Salem Center,
a friend I haven't seen in almost a year. She is not dead,
      but I guess, I am dead
to her, or she to me since we only speak in space.

The Kernwood Bridge is up, letting a boat through
      on the Danvers River. I am stuck
by the street of another friend who's gone and left, who lives across
      from a graveyard, honest, no joke.
I ask Alan would it kill someone to jump off this bridge?
      No, but you might break a few bones.

How about the Beverly Bridge? It's right there, up the river, all new
sleek, it's one of the few bridges left safe for me to drive over. *Yeah,*
that bridge will kill you. Once when we were all
friends, all alive, all clean, we ate at a clam shack there at the foot
      and saw the cops and firetrucks

screaming to the high rails. *That's not how I'd do it*, one of us said.
      And then we went back to our chowder.
How about the Veterans' Bridge over the Annisquam? I dreamed once
my car drove right over
the edge, into that warm water that would take me out
      to Wingacrsheck, and finally the Atlantic.

Oh yeah, broken into pieces, shattered. Like hitting cement, rock.
      But what are you going to do?
I want to keep asking him until I run out of bridges, all the way up
to Maine, but the call drops and my phone dies.

State of Deseret

The desert grows spiny things: cacti,
tarantulas, the diamondbacks' fangs.
And bridges grow right up from the hot red sand
and bridges are what's left
after the wind eats away at the earth. All day, I've counted up
rejection and it's a sad thing, no nobility at all. The tarot guy
(in the little shop by the big boat called "Friendship")
bade me to avoid the West. He fanned the cards I chose: a man
dangling from his foot, people jumping hand in hand
from a tower in flames, a strange queen,
a fool. The desert bridges were postcard pictures sent from a friend
I haven't seen in a long while, not even on the internet.
Or the pictures were from a friend who wanted me
to write about an alien place.
A place I've never been, never will be at.
In the state of Deseret, some men
marry forty wives. The wives pray to overcome jealousy
and hunger. I've only gone to fortune tellers when I feel mean,
and when I say mean,
I mean, I feel a broken heart, someone else's heart broken, or mine.

Prayer of the Last Baby Boomer to The Madonna de la Soccorso

Give me the tongue of Nancy Sinatra: let me truth
not lie, let me change, and not same.

Give me the cloven hooves of Satan
to walk to and fro in the earth and up and down on it.

Let me play at the table. Let me gamble on a good man's life.
Let my boots be white patent leather and fringed. Let me dance

at the bottom of the back stairs for my uncles, by the stone hibachi.
Let me dance on the horns of that old goat, the one

that is always ready to fuck, that holds the sun
between its eyes, and the moon too. Always on the cusp,

good for a joke–last spawn of the greatest generation, and boom!
this baby will grill some ribs after the wake, curse God, and die.

SHE

End of the Visible Spectrum

Red vibrates so slowly,
one has to fret. My retina stretched
to reach the garnet glass
on the table with the ruby cloth.
I was thirsty and felt
if I could drink maybe
it would be cranberry juice
or tomato juice with a splash of honest
vodka from communist
Russia. All the working girls
prefer it to the devils who own them.

Austerlitz

A bumble bee humps the bloomed clover where a young man
emerges from the mouth of the woods with a backpack full of songs.

He's looking over his shoulder for the slim-ankled love,
          the copper snake–
haired ghost, who's gone for good to the steeplebush. She put a drop

of honey on her tongue then took him in her mouth. How can he
look at anything else? Edna St.Vincent Millay had seventeen men

seventeen men in one month, some by the arborvitae by the gate.
When the bees leave, sated, and the warm lake breeze stops,
          the black mad flies

come down, one fractured idea: they beg for attention, buzz
in hair in ears at the neck.
                              He won't even swat at them–they cloud
his head until he's up and gone.

All day I've smelled almonds and roasted coffee beans
as the humidity tumbles down the hill from St. Vincent's stairwell

where (wine bottle and goblet safe at the top step) she broke
her neck her heart her love. Trees turn oaken red
          early in Austerlitz. No one even heard her fall.

Seated Figure with Hat

~ Richard Diebenkorn

We can't know if she's beautiful:
the artist painted his wife
looking away from him: the brim
of her brown fedora low over her temple,
covering the spot I test for fever
with my lips on my children, the spot
that hits the table corners always.

She is a hieroglyph: flat and all
angles: her nose under the brim,
her raised chin, a bit of black pageboy,
her breasts under her dark sleeveless shirt:
90 degrees, more or less. Maybe she is
so beautiful to him, he can't bear to paint her face or
she knows he won't eat her heart anyway
when she offers it.

She holds a glass of clear drink and
we can see through it, to her skirt,
red, and the lower steps he makes of her body:
her arm crooked on the chair, resting on its arm,
her lap, and all the blacks, the blood red, and you know
it's fall because of the layers of golden
yellow that fill the rest of the canvas. Each angle,

each V he painted, catches the overflow of color: gold
whiskey into and out from her, like the day something dies,
late in the fall's afternoon. One of them wanted a god,
one of them wanted to be a god.
In the end, nothing is ever healed by this.

Woman Making Omens on the Second Floor
(Responding to Kafka)

If, on a day of low-grade rain and siren, a woman watched
the sky lower, yellow, but had been hoping tornado; if she saw
instead, a girl-child being lured into a long gray sedan parked
kitty-corner in the schoolyard below her window, and if, as that child
called out for her mother, her arm clutched and pulled in a man's
tweed grasp, then surely, this same woman would shatter the window
with both palms, let the glass rip straight up her arm, and she would
run down, run out, arms wide, still bloody, brave, meaningful–but,

since it is true that there was no gray sedan, no girl
at all, and the maple outside her window didn't even move,
but waited, too–and though her mail, no matter how she piled it
slipped and fluttered to the floor, and a black luck spider
scuttled across the wood to her foot, and earlier, she caught her hair
in the teeth of a metal comb, then in the blow dryer's tiny motor
and burnt it out, and her coffee would not pour neatly into its cup,
grew cold and bitter, she sat, having turned from the window as if
from her own crime, and was unable to look up.

Psychopomps

The sun should rise any minute.
Some girls pray for sleep to come or more
of anything. They

will sit by the kitchen window and see
the oak: at five, they see its coat
of dead leaves, by seven, its coat of sparrows.

The Girl with Black, Black Hair and The Golden Snake

The snake is strung with drops of poison, gold
amber rosary beads,
ending with his golden eye.

*

Alabaster day, the town square blurred
by the heat of the fire
under a pot. Dust when they dragged her out.

*

*They used my pot to boil the pitch, my knife to slice
the pillows for the eider down feathers, my chair
from the kitchen. My chocolate. My cigarettes.*

*

His throat is dry, which means
his whole body is dry, even the venom.
Pitchy pine tar stings both tips of his tongue.

*

The ancient well in the middle of town
keeps the ground shady and damp. Probably there are coins
      down at the bottom.
The snake coils next to the cool stones.

*

The newsreel is black and white and captioned
collaborateur. No one in the film notices the snake by the well:
        the snake
can barely be seen, doesn't look gold.

*

The snake has cervical eyes that try to close.
That day, there are many round things: the well, the girl's mouth
when the tar poured down, a sticky mantilla of webs.

*

He can feel the yelling and someone crying so hard
under his white Jacob's Ladder belly.
The feathers wafting down were not birds.

*

A snake is like a god, exiled.
Its Jacob's Ladder belly is soft and white and feels
everything we fear.

*

What hurt most was the woman
who held my chin up
so the feathers would stick to my face.

Silhouette

~ after Kara Walker

The first one happened fast: in ancient Greece
a man was about to leave for war and he stood against
the alabaster wall of his lover's courtyard at noon.
She traced the shape of his shadow
with coal, careful to capture the bony essence: arced nose, cowlick.
What with the sun moving like a chariot, she had to trap it all.

And they are cheap! Thus, silhouette, from Etienne de Silhouette,
money minister in Paris, who urged cuts and prudence even in love—
the trick was to keep your tiny knife honed and to keep contrast.
And so, a delicate eyelash, a strong chin, a wigged man, sideways.
And silhouette, from the Basque, meaning abundance of hole
        or of cave.
And anyone with a knife could make a cave cheaply, on paper,
on the dusty layer of a shell. Anyone could make a hole.

An artist in NYC covered a whole room of white walls
        with silhouettes.
She used her X-Acto and cut skinny girls, gawky, with braids
scalloped and curved like the horns of beasts; she shaped
the noose from the tree like the braids. She cut eyelets
along the hem of a woman in a petticoat so the white
showed through the black paper and I bet she saved those
comma-shaped chads to glue around the baby dropping
from a knobby-kneed girl to make it look wet and fresh.

Sisters, Braiding

Our legs entwined, we could plait
without looking: a triple split
at the question marks our napes curved into,

tracing our spines down
to where we balanced. Our hair,
equally black, swallowed light

until it shone purple and blue, growing warm
where it entered and wound. This close
—the crook of her elbow brushing my cheek—

I could smell damp and salt and the braids would lie
slightly lapsed, like black snakes
drowsing after a good feed, the barely tamed hanks

interlocking, the thick middle, then
the left then the right—it never stood still, heating
where it joined to become braid, emerging just

where it should, slipping under and curling over again.

Dog Days

The land curves cracked and brown as an old urn.
One flat-topped squat tree still grows stubbornly.

The tree is high enough for the young girl
to dangle from a noose. She could be a wooden wind chime

if there were a breeze, she's that thin and hollow. Hungry, she had
confused food for love and approached the king:

He threw his shoe at her face. Her dog stays with her.
Under her bare feet, he crouches, maybe hoping for shade,

maybe confusing hunger for loyalty. No one will ever know
her name, but the dog

will be strung with stars in the summer sky.

Festival of the Eclipse

Through my window, I see the penumbra now: a sliver of ash, painful
as the blade of my mezzaluna. The street shines sticky with spilled
soda, melted candy. The lid of the sewer, half off, balances on the lip.
From the bottom the whole night sky is the anteumbra,
a pale eye looking down. I caused this: chopping the mint,
the oregano. And after meat,
       I bleach the oak cutting board for the blood.

When I do believe in God, I think God is simply the curve
of my mezzaluna and I rock back and forth, seeing how far
over I can go–what I mean is God is the middle moon. But then soon
after, I don't even believe that. By morning,
the street will be bone dried by the sunlight perfectly aligned between
the grid made of houses: the effect of Stonehenge.
My cutting board will be dried too, and safe
       on a flour sack. For the dolly I made during the eclipse,

I used two blue sequins from an old costume for your myopic eyes.
You hair, red lint from the angora holiday sweater I borrowed and
never returned. I'll draw the mole above your lips
with a Sharpie. An old sock for your body. No arms. No legs.
The stone keeps my mezzaluna keen in the way the salt-
filled strawberry hanging from the tomato pin cushion hones my
needles and pins
       when I push them in and out.

Stone Formations Along the Marginal Way

On the worst day since you left, I stepped off the path of the Marginal
Way into the thorny rosebushes and over the rocks to the tide pools,
which swallowed

my bare feet mercifully. I found the grayest beach stones, some
marbled with purple or pearl and started to pile the soft-edge discs
on the tip of a crag. All summer, people built

these cairns looking out to the Atlantic, hundreds and hundreds of
them, from Ogunquit to Perkins Cove, and after everybody left
for home, I made one high as my knee.

What with the wind, my hair, unkempt, blinded me on and off, but I
liked the short hollow sound of one beach stone placed on the other,
like forks against plates at an angry table.

If you came back, I'd say, *Have a bite!* if I weren't mute to you. *Look
what I made!* I'd show you my stones, squat as a woman.
She looks like us! You'd tell me I'd
buttoned my shirt wrong, one off.

Fox Sisters

I conjured her on the Ouija board.
The planchette flew from under my fingertips
and landed on the frowning crescent moon.

She wanted to write an automatic note.
She wanted to say, yes, in French. Oui.
Ja, yes, in German.

Yes, I am sorry I left you all.
Yes, you are wise to fear me.
And so Good Bye.

She'd flip the table
before showing her face.

SHE and I

The Ruins of Rievaulx Abbey

I love my mother's hair, the way it falls into a perfect page with
        with a few comb strokes
before the aricept and the seroquel and the methadone kick in and
        does she ever fight!

Still so strong! Those bony hands of hers! I inherited her thick veins:
        pipes they're called
in places where veins matter. I have her arms, too. I have
        the idea of her like the idea

of Rievaulx Abbey at the lip of an English valley: mossy oblong,
        the aisle to the nave,
its shape the shape of a church only from a distance:
        the hieroglyph of a blunted arrow.

Standing back I love how my mother's hair lies
straight and silver. When I lean in to stroke her cheek,
        she is in a deep nod.

No Face

When she has my father dial my number
to say Liz is in the living room,
I don't say: *My sister is in Texas,*
you are in your home, by the ocean.

She says she called to her, Liz,
and when she looked up, my sister
had no face. I say, *Like an egg?*

No, more like an oval hand mirror filled with smoke
she says, less frightened than by last

sundown's visitation: the seamstress in the cellar
or the one before, the men
who call her thief or the one before, the girl with no legs who floats.

I picture my sister, her face covered all around
with gray scarves or with Saran wrap.

How, Ma? How no face? She starts to cry.
My father must have taken the phone from her,
hangs it up nice and soft so

she won't get more scared and we wait
in our separate homes throughout sundown for full night.

Singer

Today, on my walk, I saw a sewing machine on the curb
across the street under the shivering locust tree. Free,

a mid-century white flip-model
you could turn over and shut into its own table. I crossed

to touch its bobbin, the throat, the tension. My mother had one,
hardly ever used, except to stitch sheets into ghosts. She wasn't

very good at sewing, nor am I nor are my sisters: we agonized
in home ec when the boys at school stayed behind to build models

and huff glue.
                When she got sick but before things
worsened, my mother saw seamstresses, hundreds of them in rows,

in the cellar, bent over fat black Singers, black
matte with gold roses painted on their bodies. 100 x 100

seamstresses and she was afraid they'd look up as one
and see her.
              My sister would say walking past this machine today
conjured my mother: a sign she is with me still. I think

of my mother and see nothing. The woman who was giving away
the Singer came out of her house, and I said

my mother had this exact Singer and she said
oh take it for her, she'll love it

and I said, no, I can't
lug it all the way back home.

A Mother of Dolls

The supply closet has: ice cream colored face cloths to fold and unfold
        and pile; Lysol
gallons of it; diapers; bins of baby dolls, full sized, undressed, with
        cloth bodies and molded plastic heads.

These babies are comforted, they never cry: the women on this floor
hold them to their chests and rock them, they mother well. They fold
        the cloths
over and over and pile. Almost all widows, they're that strong still, in
        their hearts.

*

A month or so after my mother became a widow, she picked up her
first doll.
        My father had died, baffled. I use this as a marker of time.
She was still married, or maybe not, in her mind.

*

Two women fought over a soft multi-colored pastel blanket to swaddle
        their dolls. One pulled hard, but the other held on
so that their wheelchairs rolled and swung through the rec room.

*

My sister called after a visit
        Ma has a doll.

*

The day was pastel colored: aqua sky, tangerine tiger lilies, yellow
sunlight: as I drove up the last time, I hoped she flew by
        and past me, whole.

Wives

The Madonna in the old lady's yard began to speak.
I heard this from my sister and the older girls
and by the next day, everybody knew. At first,
the things She did were good: She found lost baseballs,
stray cats, told of love and weddings, She
blessed the front yard She was in–tomatoes, roses,
and the old lady gave them away to
the people standing by the fence around the yard
who offered: bread, locks of hair, cloth
from a dead husband's suit and his watch chain,
pictures–even one on tin. Then

She told who hit the baseball through a window,
then She pointed to a man's stomach,
said, Cancer, and he got it, She spoke of the world
rolling, rolling fast toward a cliff,
and the people stopped bringing things,
but still stood by the old lady's fence.
The tomatoes and roses were left to die, she stopped
coming out, would only yell through her door
Leave me alone and then stopped that.
Someone gouged the Madonna's face with a hammer's claw.
Someone covered Her with a green plastic trash bag.
People still came. One day, all they found

was a brown circle, the size of a large face
or the full moon seen from our distance
because no one could bear this miracle:
it had to turn bad. The people thought it was done,
but She would come to my window at night
not plaster–but blue, all winter-dusk

and suffocation. I would scare my baby sister awake:
Mary's coming Mary's coming She's here–
so she would climb into my bed, and I

would hold her like she was my wife,
my hand tangled in her hair.

Picture of a Botched Abortion

~ from Our Bodies, Ourselves, *1971*

I never forgot about you, Gerri Santoro—you
in that black and white photo, in that book we all had when
        we were ten.

I knew you were dead before I knew what an abortion was, before I
        knew it could be botched.
I knew you were dead because of how still you were tucked face down
in the child's pose, in balasana (I learned that years later, in yoga class).

Your blood, sopped up in a rag, could've been any color, but I knew it
        was red, dark, I knew it
then. I knew it hurt, you were on your knees, plus I've bled out, but
not all the way like you. Not on the linoleum, not by a floorboard and
        extension cord and a plug.

I remembered you when my daughter, about two, fell asleep mid-play
in the child's pose,
        on the floor and her endless choices confounded me.
I remembered you again when I saw her spine and that quiet C of
scoliosis: I saw the bumps of your backbone too, from above,
        like the photographer did, bent.

Who would love her? Who would love her as I love her?

I remember you, Gerri Santoro, and how quiet we girls grew each time
        we flipped a page and we saw your picture.

Avocado

Good ones are ugly: dead-toad green
rough black with bumps.
When they're cheap,
my mother phones to tell me to buy.
I line them on my sill
till ripe. Yesterday,
my daughter loved
a spider scuttling over a dug up
pile of lobelia and mud: I blocked its escape
with my spade and lifted
open-palmed to her a belly
full of poison because in truth
I thought she'd be pleased.
It was black, and shone.

Orlando Poem

I watch men watch my fourteen-year-old daughter
        walk by the edge of the pool.

Her eyes look sidelong at some girls, her age, who
        watch her sidelong too.

These girls are with their mothers that no one
        watches anymore.

It is so hot here, the heat feels like sheer
        veiling edged with coins too warm to the touch
                wrapped around us all with only eyeholes.

We count up how many men watch our daughters: oh
        and the girls
                are taught no love for each other.

Feeding the Carnivorous Plant

I unwound the barbed wire
from the heart lying

all dusty in the play yard
and made a steel bouquet

for my daughter. Forgive me,
I never taught you

Jesus. And now there's pain:
acupuncture

done with the rubber milk stems
of dandelions. The albino

lashes of a baby
Venus flytrap we tried to feed

ground beef closed shut by the breath
of our fingers: eyes

too shy to accept love, sustenance. The heart's
blue tubes sent

air bullets straight through to
rooms deep in her chest: cruel

humors, weight-
less, eye-kissed.

Miacento

The albino turkeys huddle by the green barn along the Erie Canal.
They strut, the toms and the hens, pure, not beige or ecru.
Pink wattles and pink eyes take the road in sideways.
The acre or two of cabbage grown squat and low and teal looks like
the water.
        At the farmer's market in Brockport, I bought a purple
cauliflower. I had a choice of gold. I bought a slate gray pumpkin.

My daughter culled lines from five poems, choreographed a cento.
She taught three Norwegian girls the dance. The sun in Oslo is the
same as here. Around four, the sky tears down into strips of red and
        orange and indigo.

        (My mother's camel hair coat was a golden wool cigarette pelt
I never let go of.)

The Norwegians say it is not the same sun. But it is close to Oslo's.
The words of the poems delighted and confused them: *devil* and *scissors*
and *blade* and *cataracts* and *nipple* and *half moon*.

I bought a jar of honey for the pollen, vinegar from white grapes.

If I were to marry again, I'd hold this purple cauliflower blossom,
        then leave it by a granite stone.

"But the Buddha is Kind; Life is Always a Balancing Out"

I am sitting with a woman who likes me very much
at an outside cafe where they serve espresso in cups
fragile as sparrows' skulls.
I cradle my phone at my neck as I motion to her *1 minute! 1 minute!*
She smiles, plays with her silver filigree earrings.

If there's a scale inside of me that weighs the matter of things, she
is on the lighter side. The woman who called me back weighs more.
And there is no reason, or anything noble like that, to the situation.
There's no reason to bejewel elephant cows and link them trunk to tail
so they follow in a circle, acrobat balancing on their backs either.

I am grateful for getting the call back finally. The woman who likes me
very much chuckled when I rushed into the cafe late, apologizing,
apologizing, *so sorry I didn't want to blow you off again.*

Hump, or "The Weight of Life is Heavier Than Even the Weight of Things"
~Rainer Maria Rilke

There's a lady in front of me in a black shiny-as-a-hearse SmartCar.
We have to stop to let a big old turtle cross this narrow road
from the pond to the hill the men in orange vests
blow up little by little every day at noon.
The lady dangles her arm out the window.
She looks like someone in a car costume, coming home
from a party she stayed at way too long.
It's hard to know when to go
but it's good to keep things close. A man once asked me,
why don't you tie a mattress on your back?
That way, you'd never have to leave the bar.
I liked the efficiency of that, plus
I wanted another drink. The hill will be down any day now and
they will begin to build a new hill, a better one.
The lady in the tiny hearse will be home before the blasting
       and the turtle?
Explosives don't deter her: she's seen it all, carries it under her hump.

Phantom

Years later, I saw the pictures you took: that barn door, was it red
        or did you photoshop?
I know I saw it, there or later: everything else

bleached gray by the salt of the marsh on either side of
old Route 1, up in Ipswich, flat. The day we drove home south

I thought everybody should have a friend they look like, even if
they really don't, they can try, and that was you, with our cigarettes

and our black hair. Nerves ate the fat off our bones like the undead.
And the barn door was red on that splintered building, housing no
        warm thing, boards

eaten, paint gone, but a shiny door that seemed enameled to me,
something from the Orient, like a red leaf on a pile of moldy ones.

Whoever painted it locked it behind them. I never thought you cried
too much, even though I looked away when you did. I wish you had
        stayed when I turned back from the marsh.

Joan Mitchell Mulls a Possible Mandibulectomy

Only when they wanted to remove half your beautiful face
did you surrender the cigarettes
but never the booze.

Did you sit with your dead jaw on a plaid chair?
Did you jingle your options like car keys in one cupped hand
to feel the heft?

The cigarette in the other hand.
Manhattan on a cocktail napkin at your feet.
I've seen the sketches of you.

I've seen the absolute black and white sketches of you,
        everything crossed,
arms one on top of the other on your lap, skinny legs
at the knee, crossed

like fingers when we wish or lie.

Dissolution of the Soviet Union

The day the bald man was deposed, my friend overdosed and died.
The sky was yellow brown as the wheat in the Midwest
where one of three storms rolled in from. The Soviet had a beet red
birthmark on his forehead, in the shape of a South American country
and some said he purposely sank Mother Russia, in the way some said
my friend shot one bag too many on purpose. But I know–I thought
hard about this on the way to the store to buy fat white candles for the
storm–how her lips were cigarette creased like mine. That day, I
thought only of my friend and I hoped the high was a good one
and took her home
safe. There is always too much life, too much, it could
tear down walls and drown you, there's so much, you can never
measure it right.

Aphrodisiums

A fat purple pigeon roosts in the tangled branches of the white birch:
a heart protected by a ribcage. The bird is the amulet

resting on my friend's breastbone, hiding a long scar. The amulet
I see now, is a heart that holds all the secrets

of February. Something in the dark takes aim, the snow
illuminates the night, the light froze

two weeks ago, on St. Brigid's Day. The arms of the white birch
have runes carved into them: hearts and arrows so deep

the papery bark grows around them. We decide on a white ink
tattoo around her scar, white with the shiny pink rose line. The bird

heart is an amethyst so all her decisions will be sober. The snow-
light reflects off the gem's facets, gives it a tricky shape: a fist

curled around a bow, a bird, a heart. She will not eat
food cooked, just: raw oysters, chocolate. She will learn to breathe.

I

Apostrophe

Excuse me,
I'm trying to save my life.

I need to dodge the devil's stare—
he's been trying to catch my eye again.

And so, yes, I'm going to pray.

There is a star
I wish on every morning, Venus or

Lucifer the light giver. If I've wished once
on a star for you to come back, I've wished

a hundred times. If I've prayed once
in 20 sober years, I've prayed a thousand times.

And so, let's have a staring contest,

you and I, because we can't be honest.
I'll wrap this blanket around me and wish or pray.

I prayed to be rid of you.
I pray to be rid of you still.

There is no relief in any of this.

The Range

Some people crave open spaces, the range pulled
taut as a bed sheet and expectant. I got lost

driving through a town built on a flatland.
The world could have ended as it arced

miles down the highway. I aimed
straight, all the way to the horizon line.

If the heat hadn't rippled and warped
the road, I could have fallen off the edge clean.

As a Crow Flies

On my car's navigational system North Shore Road is a straight
     yellow line
between the blue of Revere Beach and the Pines River

(where a woman once walked into
and drowned herself after shooting her husband at home,
     and I thought,

what willpower, to drown oneself, to keep going farther in and under).
I am technically on Route 1 which would take me right down
     to Key West

if I kept going for days, almost as a crow flies. Airplanes lower above
     me towards Logan,
landing, so low people here need shatter-proof windows to muffle
the sound and to keep the panes whole.

They Fall Each Day, Think of It

Dollar bills, just before dawn, from the trees
that grow above the cloud cover. Lying on the curb of Bowery

and Bleecker Streets, you come to and smell quaalude crushed
on a mirror with a bad credit card. The sky becomes thick,

ready to ovulate and 57,000 magic carpets form in the mist and waft
down lower: now you see the lopped pyramids,

a silvery desert of tombs, the hummingbird eagles
twirling, George Washingtons. All silver and green,

silvery blue, mint
fresh, ready to be rolled into a straw. You shake the bills

off your shoulders, pick up your trash spike
and stab down into the loess. Fill a pillow

sham again. Swallow dry swallow whole.

Cocaine, the Last Night

The white envelope fit in my fist, and yet
I opened it eager and hopeful as a poet.

When it was empty, I slit
the plastic straw straight as a part
in dark hair and then

Emily Dickinson, all in white, walks in.
She's finally come down the steps; she thinks
something buzzes in her parlor.
But why in the world

make this decision now?
Dead, finally to come down.

She nods to me, empathic.
A shame, she says, *you didn't save*
some lines for your friends.
Now you've no one to talk to.

A Fall

March Day. Molotov.
Left struck and half-blinded in a bombed-out country.

The sun an ache in my eyes, the sun
lost in gun-gray motes.

Nobody's quick footsteps come to teach how to use my hands.
The meanings here too new, the words, rubble, Braille.

God as a Tiger in a Cage

" This tearing apart...the whole of creation is nothing but its vibration."
~ Simone Weil

Perhaps I could sit outside the cage,
push food through the bars with a broomstick
sit hungry 1,000 years
until I was thin enough with devotion,
until I disappeared.

But just to bend forward for a closer look,
the air behind me vibrates.
If I could rip out my mind,
I would.

Siren

The gridlock finally broke and I put the wreck in my rear view mirror.
      Below I saw
how the intersection was all laid out like a compass rose. To be free
from that jam felt like the drag of a cigarette after years of not, a cold
      line of blue cocaine.
To be away from that sound of the siren! I could drive so fast
it was like being deaf. Not even my radio. Not even my phone.
I always wanted it to be like flying, and it was.

Unfounded, Ungrounded

Pregnant and out of cigarettes, I walked out of the reading, off campus, down the road to the convenience store: it was July in western North Carolina, and I was getting big. Cows grazed girded by rank grasses, then a low wire fence, and beyond, the Smokey Mountains girded us all. The poems I'd been hearing made me mad–besides, it seemed OK to smoke, pregnant, in the South.

The first dead snake lay about a yard away, belly-up, not run-over, just dead, and farther down, another, both reptiles dusted copper-red, and I thought, snakes won't go where people go, but there were no people here, halfway between poetry and cigarettes. And then I thought, it's too hot even for snakes, and I remembered my mother's warning: be careful, you'll be in the South, you know.

And then the grass on my left swayed like a wave–no, no deliberate, like a flock of sparrows that rises, starts to fly, then lands. And the cows on that field moved as a single decision two steps back, ladies line-dancing, and it happened the same on my right, their meaty brains afraid, but not so afraid they raised their heads and stopped chewing.

I was cumbersome, dopey with heat, too big to run the same distance to the school or the store, so I stooped grunting to pick up a stick as long as the dead snakes. All the way down to the store, I whacked it on the ground, arms swinging over my belly, left then right, loud and raising that awful red dust.

Smoking Outside in Front of a Motion Sensor Light Because I Love My Children

I have caused the moths to come.

They want to frolic around my back porch light.

They want to kiss it.

First, they must pass around or through the spider's web

     tatted to the back porch eave.

Then, my cloud of cigarette smoke.

A good Garcia y Vega would please some gods or saints.

So, either smoke or a moth should work.

What will come of my calling you here?

Some of the moths cling to the screen door.

Some of the moths get a burning mother of a kiss.

One never makes it through the web.

The spider tears half the web to reach and swaddle him.

Half her web hangs like a torn mantilla.

Her hard work gone; her night's work well done.

Beyond it all, I'm offered a whole warm sky of stars.

The Tao of Virgil Sollozzo

Look at my veiny hands. Look at the bare trees' branches—
we're holding up the winter sky, giving it back its darkness.

A pack of menthol cigarettes, a half empty bic lighter;
cleaned out clam shell found on the beach by the stone calendar.

In the movie, the doomed cop said I've frisked 1000 young punks.
My daughter's name scrawled, my son's, on the back
        of an old ticket stub.

No love is lighter than the rocks on the beach.
No love outlasts graphite or lead.

The I Ching instructs us how to live without blame.
How to pass through a window earthen vessels filled
        with rice and wine.

But where to find the best veal in the city?
Where to get a guarantee?
Have I yet missed my chance? I am not yet the hunted one.
My hands are empty, see?

The Devil Tides

There are rocks off the coast shaped like eggs. There are rocks shaped like misery and one like a skull. Bodies have washed up on the slippery barnacles at low tide. There is a brown island I can walk to from the crushed shell beach. If you are born up here, you know sadness and you know gulls. You know how a good clamshell makes a good ashtray. You know the land is as flat as any place where men change into wolves under the mutton moon. You know that. Resent everything, for it's the only way you don't forget. Resent everything you love, it keeps you anchored to the beach. Fishing boats bring in cargo from pink and white tulip fields in the Orient. The heroin is cheap and it is hot. Just past King's Beach the seaweed is red clogged with pennies or fingers. It smells even in the cold. Too many villages are connected by thin causeways pinched on either side by the Atlantic. Devil tides cut them off from the world. Folks go out and never come back. There are empty graves engraved in marble in big churches. Folks go out hot and turn blue. No one ever forgets, except how to measure. If you knew this, you'd never ask anything more of me.

Ultrasound of a Ghost

Echo on a screen, milky constellation, fossil shape of stars
dead before all the oceans and the sun: why

name you a name? I listen for your heart, I hear
the voice of chastisement: oh you can't have nice things.

No woman was made to name anything. I may as well go out tonight
with my Star Gazer's Guide to tap each inflorescence that stalks

the path from our home to the field and beyond
to the mountain: Arrow, I'll name one, Northern Cross, Twins

Wolf. No woman was made to name, but I do lie: there are no
blue flowers, no flowers of any kind just the old

swing set, rusty chained, twisted blown, crying, crying.

After God

Outside, the neighbor's dog barks madly at a sparrow
in the maple, and the same breeze

moving through its expectant limbs abrades my arms.
Even my hands seem weighty things curled

in my lap. The silver barrette, clasping my hair
away from my neck, tugs,

and any worry–the basil needs water, we need milk,
the wood floors need a sweep, the heat's

warped the windows again and they won't ever shut–
is as bothersome as sweat.

I should keep still today. Let the bugs in if they want,
not think of the ocean. Useless work. I mean now,

after God, to give meaning to any of this,
to name it, or fix it, or love it.

Mal 'Occhio

The red pepper hangs from a nail
above the back doorjamb, and the totem

inside its belly laughs–he is rich, hunchback
and can trick the Devil. I take careful

stock, touch my stoneware
plates, the ones with fired apples

on ivory paint. The white ceramic bowl
with spare change and spare keys. Unfinished

crewelwork blessing in its bag. The needles. Books.
Here is where I pray at night,

the foot of my bed. This is my coverlet,
undyed muslin and clean. And under it,

a brutal thing, an ugly girl,
God-blessed, left alone. The ceiling

shines white, drinking up what little
moon can come through: a cup of milk, enough

for one night. That's it. No one wants
anything of mine. I don't even make

a shadow on the wall. The bedsprings barely
creak as I pull the pure cotton

close and tight, gift-wrapped, like a nun.
Muffled goodness. Beneficent abstraction. Snuffed flame.

White Birches

".....when the Erinyes were about to put Orestes out of his mind, they appeared to him black, but once he had bitten off his finger they appeared to be white...."

It is a pleasure to walk through the gem-tone-
theme of my neighborhood streets: Emerald, Sapphire, and my own,
Ruby. One home has a small forest
of white birch trees, straight with bark fragile as
rolling papers, and there is peace in that spot
every season, no matter what: the color never changes and
the house is quiet like someone inside was dancing and stopped.

There's a small strip of stores at the top of the street—a package store,
a deli, a bank. The end of my tiny trek
could be in any one of those shops—the end of yours, too,
if you've already fallen, if the decision has been made,
you could fill a tote bag with whiskey or candy or rope
for a noose, money, you could gamble. The walk back home
past the white birch forest is best: my tote's still full and
even though I see my shoes move, they don't make a sound.

Notes

"Elysian" –Inspired by Marie Howe

"Pumpjacks in Iran"–This is my homage to the excellent film by Ana Lily Amirpour, *A Girls Walks Home Alone At Night*, which chronicles the events of an Iranian vampire in Bad City. I saw this as a love story.

"Tree"–This is a response to Danez Smith's essay, "Open Letter to White Poets" written after the horror of Ferguson, where he asks, "What frees you to write odes of the low country of America, to mention the trees…?"

"Evil Fields"–In March, 2013, Jeff Bush was swallowed by a sink hole which opened up under his bedroom, in Tampa, Florida. In ancient Rome, Vestal Virgins (priestesses committed to the goddess Vesta) were charged with keeping the holy fires lit and remaining chaste. If they broke their vow of chastity, they were buried alive.

"Wreaths the Elected Wear"–This poem references Nic Cage in *The Wicker Man*, Tessie in Shirley Jackson's *The Lottery*, and Roberto Calasso's *The Marriage of Cadmus and Harmony*.

"Belshazzar's Feast"–In the story of Daniel, a disembodied hand appeared at the feast of King Bleshazzar, "writing on the wall"– "MENE MENE TEKEL PARSIN"–meaning "God has numbered the days of your kingdom and has brought them to an end; you have been weighed and found wanting; the kingdom is divided and given to the Mendes and the Persians."

"State of Deseret"–Deseret was the name of Utah, as a territory. It derived from the word for "honeybees" in the Book of Mormon.

"Fox Sisters"–Leah, Margaret and Kate Fox were three women in the Spiritualist movement of the 1800's. They later confessed to being hoaxes and died in poverty.

"But the Buddha is Kind; Life is Always a Balancing Out"–This quote is taken from Melanie Thernstrom's book, *Halfway Heaven: Diary of a Harvard Murder* (Plume: 1998), which chronicles the 1995 murder-suicide of Sinedu Tadesse and Trang Phung Ho, juniors at Harvard University. The line is taken from Trang's memorial service.

"Hump, or *The Weight of Life is Heavier Than Even the Weight of Things*"– from Rilke's poem, "The Neighbor."

"Joan Mitchell Mulls a Possible Mandibulectomy"–A mandibulectomy is the surgical removal of all or part of the jawbone, usually as a treatment for cancer.

"They Fall, Each Day, Think of It"–Even if unemployed, Mitt Romney would make 57,000.00 a day. If one were to lay out 57,000 one dollar bills, it would take sixteen hours to pick them all up. And then you'd have to do it the next day. And the next.

"Fear of Castration…The Uncanny Valley" is a hypothesis in the field of aesthetics which holds that when features look and move almost, but not exactly, like natural beings, it causes a response of revulsion among some observers. The "valley" refers to the dip in a graph of the comfort level of beings as subjects move toward a healthy, natural likeness.

"Woman Making Omens"–This is a response to Franz Kafka's "Up the in Gallery."

"Tao of Virgil Sollozzo"–Virgil "The Turk" Sollozzo was a character in Mario Puzo's *The Godfather*. He is shot dead at Louis' Restaurant (best veal in the city) by Michael Corleone. This marks Michael's transformation, his embracing of "The Family."

"Mal'Occhio"–An Italian curse, meaning "evil eye."

Some of the poems in *The Uncanny Valley* have appeared previously:

After the Pause : "Feeding the Carnivorous Plant"
Apeiron Review: "The Tao of Virgil Sollozzo"
Broadsided Press: "State of Deseret"
The Bellingham Review: "After God"
Bitterzoet: "White Birches"
Bop Dead City: "Picture of a Botched Abortion"
Burntdistrict: "Seated Figure with Hat"
The Chiron Review: "[the heart dies without space for love, without a
    moral horizon]"
Calliope: "Wives" (Sue Elkind Poetry Finalist)
Cactus Heart: "A Mother of Dolls"
The Compassion Anthology: "Dissolution of the Soviet Union"
Echolocation: Doubles Anthology: "Stone Formations Along the
    Marginal Way"
Ekphrastic: "Silhouette"
East Coast Literary Review: "The Mountain, 1971"
Folio: "Woman Making Omens on the Second Floor"
Gargoyle Review:"Strep" (as "Pete Townshend's Voice Behind Me
    and the Snowplow's Blade Before Me")
Hermeneutic Chaos: "At the End of the Visible Spectrum"
Incessant Pipe: "Fear of Going Blind is the Fear of Castration" and
    "Prayer of the Last Baby Boomer to the Madonna de la Soccorso"
The Inflectionist Review: "A Fall"
Jersey Devil Press: "The Girl with Black, Black Hair and the
    Golden Snake"
Kalliope: "Sisters, Braiding"
Kindred: "Similes After a Quick Thaw and a Cold Snap" and
    "The Ruins of Rievaulx Abbey"
The Lindenwood Review: "The Devil Tides"(winner, prose poetry contest)
Menacing Hedge: "Austerlitz"
Mississippi Review: "Cocaine, the Last Night"
The Mom Egg: "Colostrum" and "No Face"
Monarch Review: "Bomb"
A Narrow Fellow: "Elysian" and "Evil Fields"
Naugatuck River Review: "Peasant's Pie, Devil's Tooth"
Paper Nautilus : "Thistle, Blue" and "Ultrasound of a Ghost"
Poemeleon: "Supper During Watergate" and "The Veiled Women"

Petrichor Machine: "Unfounded, Ungrounded," "But the Buddha is Kind; Life is Always a Balancing Out," and "Paean"

Red Paint Hill Journal : "Festival of the Eclipse"

Right Hand Pointing: "Dog Days," "The Range," "Joan Mitchell Mulls a Possible Mandibulectomy," "Psychopomps, (published as "Some Girls")," "Hump," "Asexuality," "Orlando," and "Heaviness"

Rust+Moth: "Ananke"

Rogue Agent : "Tit"

The Screech Owl : "Mr. Golub's Death"

Slippery Elm: "As a Crow Flies," "God as a Tiger in a Cage," and "On Sex Chromosomes and Co-Dependency"

Spry: "At a Crowded Party, I am not Envious"

82 Review: "Day of Atonement"

Stone Boat: "Wrists"

Sugared Water: "Avocado"

The Stray Branch : "Siren"

3Elements Review: "Honeymoon at the End of the Eighties"

Tar River Poetry: "Incus. Malleus. Stapes."

The Tishman Review: "Aphrodisiums"

Up the Staircase Quarterly: "Tree"

Wherewithal: "Pumpjacks in Iran"

Yellow Chair Review: "Fox Sisters"

ZigZag Folio: "Peace and Trust Can Win the Day Despite of All Your Losing" (published as "Invasion")

Outsiders, an Anthology: 'Mal 'Occhio"

"Mal'Occhio," "The Range," "White Birches," "After God" and "Smoking Outside in Front of a Motion Sensor Light Because I Love My Children," were re-printed and re-mixed in *Poetry Storehouse*.

Some of the poems in this collection were published in a chapbook, *Apostrophe*, by Big Table Publishing Company.

Acknowledgements

Thank you to The Salem Writers' Group. Thank you Jennifer Jean, Cindy Veach, January Gill O'Neil. Thank you Incessant Pipe, Clay Ventre and M.P. Carver. Thank you Warren Wilson M.F.A. Program for Writers, my teachers, and especially my pretzels: Barbara O'Dair, Brandel France de Bravo, Crystal Bacon, Laure-Anne Bosselaar. And thank you, Robin Stratton, for your patience and love.

About the Author

Jennifer Martelli attended Boston University and The Warren Wilson M.F.A. Program for Writers. She's taught both high school and college. A recipient of the Massachusetts Cultural Council Grant in Poetry, she is an associate editor for *The Compassion Anthology*. Jennifer Martelli lives in Marblehead, Massachusetts with her family.

40367253R00073

Made in the USA
Middletown, DE
10 February 2017